2·3

Animals and Their Senses/
Los sentidos de los animales

ANIMAL TASTE/
EL GUSTO EN LOS ANIMALES

by/por Kirsten Hall

Reading consultant/Consultora de lectura: Susan Nations, M.Ed.,
author, literacy coach, consultant/autora, tutora de alfabetización, consultora

WR WEEKLY READER
EARLY LEARNING LIBRARY™

Please visit our web site at: www.earlyliteracy.cc
For a free color catalog describing Weekly Reader® Early Learning Library's list
of high-quality books, call 1-877-445-5824 (USA) or 1-800-387-3178 (Canada).
Weekly Reader® Early Learning Library's fax: (414) 336-0164.

Library of Congress Cataloging-in-Publication Data available upon request from the publisher.
Fax (414) 336-0157 for the attention of the Publishing Records Department.

ISBN 0-8368-4817-9 (lib. bdg.)
ISBN 0-8368-4823-3 (softcover)

This North American edition first published in 2006 by
Weekly Reader® Early Learning Library
A Member of the WRC Family of Companies
330 West Olive Street, Suite 100
Milwaukee, WI 53212 USA

Weekly Reader® Early Learning Library Editor: Barbara Kiely Miller
Weekly Reader® Early Learning Library Art Direction: Tammy West
Weekly Reader® Early Learning Library Graphic Designer and Page Layout: Jenni Gaylord
Weekly Reader® Early Learning Library Translators: Tatiana Acosta and Guillermo Gutiérrez

Photo Credits
The publisher would like to thank the following for permission to reproduce their royalty-free photographs:
AbleStock: 4, 6, 7; Brand X Pictures: 5; Corel: 15, 16, 19; Digital Vision: cover, title page, 8, 9, 11, 13, 14, 17, 18, 20; Fotosearch/Brand X Pictures: 12; Fotosearch/Corbis: 21; Fotosearch/Image Source: 10

Printed in the United States of America

1 2 3 4 5 6 7 8 9 09 08 07 06 05

Note to Educators and Parents

Reading is such an exciting adventure for young children! They are beginning to integrate their oral language skills with written language. To encourage children along the path to early literacy, books must be colorful, engaging, and interesting; they should invite the young reader to explore both the print and the pictures.

Animals and Their Senses is a new series designed to help children read about the five senses in animals. In each book young readers will learn interesting facts about the bodies of some animals and how the featured sense works for them.

Each book is specially designed to support the young reader in the reading process. The familiar topics are appealing to young children and invite them to read — and reread — again and again. The full-color photographs and enhanced text further support the student during the reading process.

In addition to serving as wonderful picture books in schools, libraries, homes, and other places where children learn to love reading, these books are specifically intended to be read within an instructional guided reading group. This small group setting allows beginning readers to work with a fluent adult model as they make meaning from the text. After children develop fluency with the text and content, the book can be read independently. Children and adults alike will find these books supportive, engaging, and fun!

— Susan Nations, M.Ed., author/literacy coach/reading consultant

Nota para los educadores y los padres

¡Leer es una aventura tan emocionante para los niños pequeños! A esta edad están comenzando a integrar su manejo del lenguaje oral con el lenguaje escrito. Para animar a los niños en el camino de la lectura incipiente, los libros deben ser coloridos, estimulantes e interesantes; deben invitar a los jóvenes lectores a explorar la letra impresa y las ilustraciones.

Los sentidos de los animales es una nueva colección diseñada para que los niños lean textos sobre los cinco sentidos en los animales. En cada libro, los jóvenes lectores aprenderán datos interesantes del cuerpo de algunos animales y cómo éstos usan el sentido que se presenta.

Cada libro está especialmente diseñado para ayudar a los jóvenes lectores en el proceso de lectura. Los temas familiares llaman la atención de los niños y los invitan a leer — y releer — una y otra vez. Las fotografías a todo color y el tamaño de la letra ayudan aún más al estudiante en el proceso de lectura.

Además de servir como maravillosos libros ilustrados en escuelas, bibliotecas, hogares y otros lugares donde los niños aprenden a amar la lectura, estos libros han sido especialmente concebidos para ser leídos en un grupo de lectura guiada. Este contexto permite que los lectores incipientes trabajen con un adulto que domina la lectura mientras van determinando el significado del texto. Una vez que los niños dominan el texto y el contenido, el libro puede ser leído de manera independiente. ¡Estos libros les resultarán útiles, estimulantes y divertidos a niños y a adultos por igual!

— Susan Nations, M.Ed., autora/tutora de alfabetización/consultora de desarrollo de la lectura

People taste food with their **tongues**. Our tongues have little bumps on them. The bumps are called **taste buds**.

— — — — — — — — —

Las personas percibimos el sabor de la comida con la **lengua**. Nuestra lengua tiene pequeños bultitos. Estos bultitos se llaman **papilas gustativas**.

4

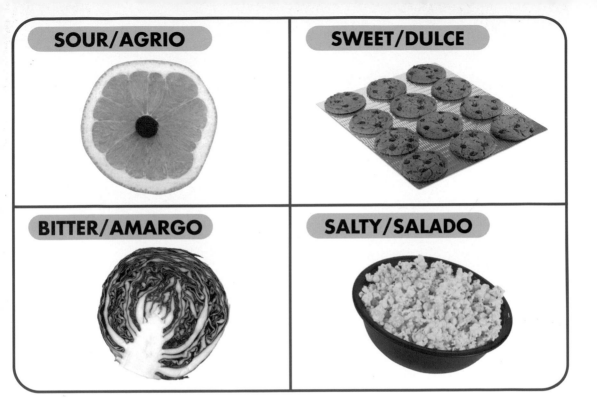

| SOUR/AGRIO | SWEET/DULCE |
| BITTER/AMARGO | SALTY/SALADO |

Taste buds help us know how foods taste. They tell us if foods taste sour, sweet, bitter, or salty.

Las papilas gustativas nos ayudan a conocer el sabor de la comida. Nos dicen si algo tiene un sabor agrio, dulce, amargo o salado.

Rabbits have about twice as many taste buds as people do. Grass must taste good to rabbits.

- - - - - - - -

Los conejos tienen casi dos veces más papilas gustativas que los humanos. La hierba les debe saber rico.

Birds do not have many taste buds. Maybe that is why they are not picky about what they eat!

■ ■ ■ ■ ■ ■ ■ ■ ■

Los pájaros no tienen muchas papilas gustativas. ¡Quizá por eso no son muy exigentes con la comida!

Apes eat sweet foods, such as bananas. They also eat bitter plants — leaves, tree bark, and flowers.

Los simios comen cosas dulces como las bananas. También comen cosas amargas — hojas, cortezas de árbol y flores.

Flies eat sweet foods, too. They do not eat foods that taste bitter.

— — — — — — — —

Las moscas también comen cosas dulces. No comen cosas con sabor amargo.

Pigs eat foods that taste bitter. They eat bitter grasses and vegetables.

- - - - - - - - -

Los cerdos comen cosas con sabor amargo. Comen hierbas y verduras amargas.

bamboo/
bambú

Pandas eat **bamboo** all day long. Bamboo has a
bitter taste.

- - - - - - - -

Los pandas pasan el día comiendo **bambú**. El bambú tiene
sabor amargo.

Dogs eat mostly meat. Many meats have a salty taste.

- - - - - - - -

Los perros comen sobre todo carne. Muchas carnes tienen sabor salado.

Cats can taste salty, bitter, and sour flavors. They cannot taste sweet foods very well.

- - - - - - - -

Los felinos pueden percibir el sabor salado, el amargo y el agrio. No pueden percibir lo dulce muy bien.

roof/cielo

A snake does not taste food with its tongue. It tastes with the **roof**, or top, of its mouth.

- - - - - - - -

La serpiente no percibe el sabor de la comida con la lengua. Lo hace con el **cielo**, o parte superior, de la boca.

A crocodile does not taste with its tongue, either. It also tastes with the roof of its mouth.

- - - - - - - - -

El cocodrilo tampoco percibe el sabor con la lengua. Lo hace también con el cielo de la boca.

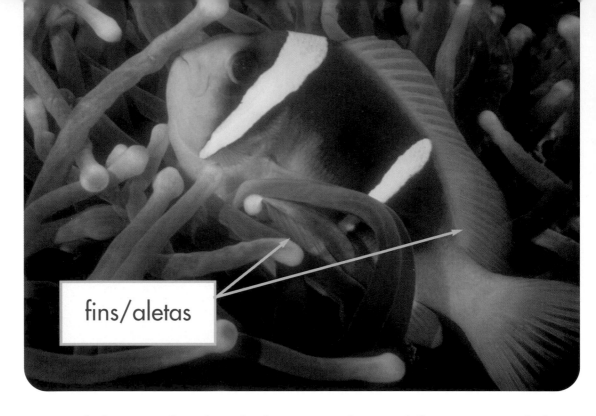

fins/aletas

Many fish taste food with their mouths and fins. Some fish can even taste with their tails.

- - - - - - - - -

Muchos peces perciben el sabor con la boca y con las aletas. Algunos pueden percibir el sabor hasta con la cola.

Butterflies taste with their feet. They use their tongues like straws to sip liquids from flowers.

■ ■ ■ ■ ■ ■ ■ ■ ■

Las mariposas perciben el sabor con las patas. Usan la lengua como un popote para sorber el líquido de las flores.

antennae/
antenas

Ants feel around with their **antennae** to find food. They taste with their antennae, too.

Las hormigas buscan la comida con las **antenas**. Con sus antenas también perciben el sabor.

Beetles also taste with their antennae. Most beetles eat plants and flowers.

- - - - - - - - -

Los escarabajos también perciben el sabor con las antenas. La mayoría come plantas y flores.

All animals need food and water to live. But food or water that tastes bad may make animals sick.

— — — — — — — —

Todos los animales necesitan comida y agua para vivir. Pero pueden enfermarse si comen o beben algo con sabor a podrido.

The sense of taste is important for animals. It helps them know which foods to eat to stay healthy.

━ ━ ━ ━ ━ ━ ━ ━ ━

El sentido del gusto es importante para los animales. Los ayuda a saber qué pueden comer para no enfermarse.

Glossary

antennae — feelers; thin movable body parts on the heads of some insects

bamboo — a plant with a hollow stem and bitter-tasting leaves

taste buds — bumps on the tongue that send messages to the brain about taste

tongue — the large piece of flesh attached to the bottom of the mouths of people and many animals

Glosario

antenas — partes delgadas y flexibles que tienen en la cabeza algunos insectos

bambú — planta de tallo hueco y hojas amargas

lengua — órgano carnoso y alargado que está pegado a la parte inferior de la boca de las personas y de muchos animales

papilas gustativas — abultamientos en la lengua que envían al cerebro información sobre los sabores

For More Information/Más información

Books

Animal Mouths. Look Once, Look Again (series).
David M. Schwartz (Gareth Stevens)

Munching, Crunching, Sniffing and Snooping. Eyewitness
Readers (series). Brian Moses (DK Publishing)

Libros

Pigs/Los cerdos. Animals That Live on the Farm/
Animales que viven en la granja (series).
JoAnn Early Macken (Weekly Reader Early Learning Library)

La mariposa monarca. Cyclos de vida (series).
David M Schwartz (Gareth Stevens)

Index

Índice

About the Author

Kirsten Hall is an author and editor. While she was still in high school, she published her first book for children, *Bunny, Bunny*. Since then she has written and published more than eighty titles. A former teacher, Kirsten currently spends her days writing and editing and her evenings tutoring. She lives in New York City with her husband.

Información sobre la autora

Kirsten Hall es escritora y editora. Publicó su primer libro para niños, *Bunny, Bunny*, cuando aún asistía a la escuela secundaria. Desde entonces, ha escrito y publicado más de ochenta títulos. Kirsten, que anteriormente fue maestra, pasa el día escribiendo y editando, y por la noche da clases. Kirsten vive en la ciudad de Nueva York con su esposo.